Backyard Animals
Salamanders

Nick Winnick

Weigl Publishers Inc.

Published by Weigl Publishers Inc.
350 5th Avenue, Suite 3304, PMB 6G
New York, NY 10118-0069
Website: www.weigl.com

Library of Congress Cataloging-in-Publication Data

Winnick, Nick.
 Salamanders / Nick Winnick.
    p. cm. -- (Backyard animals)
 Includes index.
 ISBN 978-1-60596-084-5 (hard cover : alk. paper) -- ISBN 978-1-60596-085-2 (soft
cover : alk. paper)
 1. Salamanders--Juvenile literature. I. Title.

 QL668.C2W56 2010
 597.8'5--dc22

                                    2008052060

Printed in China
1 2 3 4 5 6 7 8 9 0 13 12 11 10 09

Editor Heather C. Hudak
Design Terry Paulhus

All of the Internet URLs given in the book were valid at the time of publication.
However, due to the dynamic nature of the Internet, some addresses may have
changed, or sites may have ceased to exist since publication. While the author
and publisher regret any inconvenience this may cause readers, no responsibility
for any such changes can be accepted by either the author or the publisher.

Photo Credits

Weigl acknowledges Getty Images as its primary image supplier for this title.

Contents

Meet the Salamander

Salamanders are amphibians. Amphibians are animals that live both in water and on land. They have smooth skin and are cold-blooded. Salamanders are closely related to frogs.

Salamanders have several ways of breathing. Some use **gills**. Others use lungs or breathe through their skin. Some salamanders change the way they breathe as they get older.

Most often, salamanders are found near water. Most have powerful tails to help them swim, and some have webbed feet. Salamanders cannot survive in salt water.

The smallest salamanders are less than 1 inch (2.5 centimeters) in length.

Salamanders move using the same kind of side-to-side wriggle that a snake does.

All about Salamanders

Salamanders, frogs, and **caecilians** are the only kinds of amphibians living today. Salamanders are different from other amphibians because they have tails. The long, thin body of a salamander looks very similar to that of a lizard.

Most salamanders are small, but some, such as hellbenders, tigers, and mudpuppies, can grow to be about 1 to 2 feet (31 to 61 cm) in length. The largest salamanders grow to be 5 to 6 feet (1.5 to 1.8 meters) long.

Unlike noisy frogs, salamanders are very quiet and often hard to find.

V'here Salamanders Live

Rough-skinned Newt
- Lives along the west coast of the United States and Canada

Mudpuppy
- Found in the northeastern United States and parts of Canada

Tiger Salamander
- Lives throughout the United States, southern Canada, and eastern Mexico

Hellbender
- Found in the eastern United States

Salamander History

Almost 400 million years ago, a type of fish was **adapting** to life on dry land. Some scientists believe that these fish hunted **prey** that lived along ancient shorelines. They waited under the water, snapping at prey that came close by. Over a long time, these fish began to spend more time on land to avoid **predators**. They developed legs and lungs, and left the water behind.

Early amphibians looked quite different from the ones on Earth today. Their modern cousins still spend a great deal of time in and near the water.

Some early amphibians had scales and body armor.

The bones in the arms and legs of salamanders are made up of the same basic parts as those of humans.

Salamander Shelter

Most often, salamanders live in cool, rainy places, where there is plenty of moisture. They prefer forests, ponds, and streams, but can survive in dry areas. Some even live in trees. Salamanders can only live in fresh water. Salt water is **poisonous** to most amphibians.

Salamanders can be found on most continents, except Australia or Antarctica. Most states are home to at least one kind of salamander. They are very common in the Appalachian Mountains in eastern North America, where the weather is **humid**. Fewer types of salamanders live in dry areas, such as Utah, Montana, and Nevada.

One-third of all the world's salamanders live in North America.

Hellbenders are the largest salamanders in North America.

Salamander Features

All salamanders share the same basic features. Their bodies are specially adapted to help them live both in water and on land.

EYES
Salamanders have poor eyesight. Their eyes work the same whether they are in water or on land.

SKIN
A salamander's skin absorbs oxygen. This helps it breathe underwater.

TEETH
Salamander teeth are curved inward like hooks. This keeps their prey from escaping.

GILLS
Young salamanders breathe through gills. Most grow lungs later in life. Some salamanders keep their gills their whole lives.

TAIL
A salamander's tail helps the salamander to move through water and over land.

What Do Salamanders Eat?

Salamanders, and all other amphibians, are **carnivores**. They mainly eat insects, but sometimes eat lizards, rodents, and other amphibians.

Salamanders have sticky tongues that stick to small prey. Muscles in a salamander's throat squeeze around a bone called the hyoid. As the hyoid is squeezed, it pops forward, shooting the salamander's tongue toward its prey. This happens very fast, often catching the prey by surprise. Other muscles in the salamander's body reel its tongue back in, carrying the prey into its mouth.

The muscles that pull a salamander's tongue back into its mouth are attached to its back legs.

Sharks feed in a similar way to salamanders, but they shoot their whole lower jaw forward.

Salamander Life Cycle

Most salamanders begin their lives in the water. Their eggs do not have hard shells like lizards or birds. For this reason, the eggs need to be laid near water, or they will dry out. Some salamanders lay their eggs in clumps under

Eggs

Most salamanders start their lives as small, jelly-like eggs. The yolk in the middle of the egg contains the **nutrients** the baby salamander needs to grow. The yolk is protected by a thick layer of jelly. A female salamander will lay many eggs at once. This ensures that at least some of the young salamanders survive.

Young Salamanders

Young salamanders are different from adults in many ways. They mainly live in the water and have gills to breathe, instead of lungs. Many have webbed feet to help them swim. A few have no arms or legs at all. They grow limbs when they become adults.

water. Others lay eggs on the undersides of leaves hanging over a pond or stream. This way, when an egg hatches, the young salamander drops straight into the water.

Adult Salamanders

Most salamanders go through **metamorphosis** before they become adults. They lose their gills and grow lungs. This lets them spend more time on land. Some salamanders only become adults after spending the winter **hibernating**. This is rare.

Encountering Salamanders

When salamanders are not hunting or looking for a mate, they spend much of their time hiding. They prefer cool, dark places, and tend to hide under bushes, in rotting logs, and in burrows. Salamanders are mostly nocturnal animals. This means they are most active at night. Some groups hibernate during dry or cold seasons. They become active again in warmer, wetter weather.

People should never try to touch or grab a salamander. They have very soft bodies and can be harmed by the heat and oils of human hands. If you see one of these gentle creatures, be sure to watch it from a distance.

Useful Websites

To learn more about salamanders, visit www.sandiegozoo.org/animalbytes/t-salamander.html.

Some people study salamanders in nature. Never catch a wild salamander to keep as a pet.

Myths and Legends

There are many legends around the world about salamanders. These stories have been told for many years.

In ancient times, people thought salamanders were creatures of fire. Salamanders often sleep and hibernate in dead logs. When people put these logs into a fire, the salamanders would scurry away from the heat. People thought the fire was making the salamanders.

Many stories grew about these creatures. Some people thought salamanders could live in and put out fires. Some early Jewish writings said that salamander blood could keep a person safe from fire.

C. S. Lewis wrote a series of children's books called *The Chronicles of Narnia*. In the book *The Silver Chair*, the main characters meet a group of salamanders. The salamanders use their wisdom to help the characters escape evil creatures that are chasing them.

In cartoons, books, and movies, salamanders often appear as fire-breathing creatures.

A Salamander Legend

People living on the Asahi river in Japan tell a story about a giant salamander who lived in Ryuto-ga-fuchi. *This means "Dragon's Head Abyss."*

At one time, all people avoided the abyss. When the water there was disturbed, the salamander would thrash around and swallow the person who caused it to stir. A young man named Hikoshiro Mitsui dove into the abyss with a short sword in his teeth. He hoped to defeat the salamander. Hikoshiro was swallowed alive, but he cut his way out of the beast's belly.

The giant salamander was angry. It made awful noises and threatened the village for many nights. One day, the people of the village raised a shrine to honor the salamander. They called it *Hanzaki Daimyojin* or Lord Salamander. The shrine still stands as a reminder to leave salamanders alone and to protect the places where they sleep.

Frequently Asked Questions

Do salamanders have any enemies?

Answer: Salamanders are often eaten by skunks, shrews, snakes, birds, frogs, and even other salamanders. Humans are another threat to salamanders. Human activity is destroying their homes in nature.

Can salamanders protect themselves from enemies?

Answer: Yes. Some salamanders have poisonous chemicals on their skin. These chemicals make them taste bad to predators.

How long will a pet salamander live?

Answer: Tiger salamanders, a popular kind of pet salamander, can live up to 20 years. They live 12 to 15 years in nature.

Puzzler

See if you can answer these questions about salamanders.

1. What kind of water is poisonous to salamanders?
2. How long ago did the first amphibians start to walk on land?
3. What are the only kinds of amphibians living today?
4. What makes a salamander egg different from reptile and bird eggs?
5. Which bone in the salamander's body helps shoot its tongue out to catch prey?

Answers: 1. salt water **2.** 400 million years ago **3.** salamanders, frogs, and caecilians **4.** Salamander eggs do not have hard shells. **5.** the hyoid bone

Find Out More

There are many more interesting facts to learn about salamanders. Look for these and other books at your library.

Petranka, J. W. *Salamanders U.S. & Canada*. Smithsonian, 1998.

Miller, Sara Swan. *Salamanders: Secret, Silent Lives*. Franklin Watts, 2000.

Words to Know

adapting: a type of animal changing its form over a long time

caecilians: amphibians that are long and worm-like

carnivores: animals that eat only other animals

gills: organs that an animal uses to breathe underwater

hibernating: spending the winter sleeping

humid: wet or moist

metamorphosis: a major change in an animal when it becomes an adult

nutrients: provides the food and energy an animal needs to grow

poisonous: can cause sickness or death

predators: animals that hunt other animals for food

prey: animals that are hunted by other animals for food

Index